# GARBAGE
## AND
# RECYCLING

### ROSIE HARLOW & SALLY MORGAN

## KINGFISHER
### NEW YORK

KINGFISHER
LONDON & NEW YORK

Text copyright © Macmillan Publishers International Ltd 1995
Published in the United States by Kingfisher, 175 Fifth Ave., New York, NY 10010
Kingfisher is an imprint of Macmillan Children's Books, London.
All rights reserved.

Distributed in the U.S. and Canada by Macmillan, 175 Fifth Ave., New York, NY 10010

LIBRARY OF CONGRESS CATALOGING-IN-PUBLICATION DATA
Harlow, Rosie.
Garbage and recycling / Rosie Harlow, Sally Morgan.—1st ed.
p. cm.—(Young discoverers)
Includes bibliographical references and index.
1. Refuse and refuse disposal—Juvenile literature.
2. Recycling (waste etc.)—Juvenile literature.
[1. Refuse and refuse disposal. 2. Recycling (Waste)].
I. Morgan, Sally. II. Title. III. Series.
TD792.N373    1995
363.72'8—dc20  95-6371  CIP AC

ISBN: 978-0-7534-5503-6

Kingfisher books are available for special promotions and premiums. For details contact:
Special Markets Department, Macmillan, 175 Fifth Avenue, New York, NY 10010.

For more information, please visit www.kingfisherbooks.com

Printed in China
16
16TR/0317/WKT/(RNB)/128MA/F

Illustrations: Julian Baker cover, p. 10 (left), 12 (left), 24 (top); Peter Bull p. 5 (top), 8, 9, 11 (bottom), 16 (bottom), 18, 21, 26 (bottom), 27, 28 (left and top); Richard Draper p. 22, 30; Deborah Kindred p. 7 (top), 13, 14 (top); Janos Marffy p. 7 (bottom), 14–15, 17 (bottom), 23, 24 (bottom), 28 (right), 29; Mike Saunders p. 4–5 (bottom), 12 (right), 17 (top), 20, 25; Ian Thompson p. 6, 19; Richard Ward p. 4 (top), 10–11, 16 (top), 31Photographs: 13 Alamy/A Howden; 26 Alamy/Mira; all other images iStock.

# About This Book

This book looks at the problems of producing too much garbage and explains how recycling can help to make our environment a cleaner and safer place. It suggests lots of experiments and things to look out for, as well as ways to reduce, reuse, and recycle our waste.

You should be able to find nearly everything you need for the experiments in and around your home. Be sure to wear rubber gloves whenever you are handling garbage or litter.

## Activity Hints

- Before you begin an experiment, read through the instructions carefully and collect all the things you need.
- When you have finished, clear everything away, especially sharp scissors, and wash your hands.
- Start a special notebook so you can keep a record of what you do in each experiment and the things you find out.

# Contents

# What a Waste!

People produce loads of garbage. Throughout the world, we create a billion tons of it each year. Even cavemen produced it. Their caves soon filled with old bones, wood, and other waste, so eventually they had to move to a new cave. Today, we create more garbage than ever before. But many of the things we think of as garbage are not waste at all. They are made from valuable materials taken from the environment (called raw materials) that *could* be used again.

## Wasted Cars

In the United States, over seven million cars are scrapped each year. The metal can be recycled, but that still leaves waste, including a lot of tires!

restaurant waste

litter

garage waste

household waste

Instead of being thrown away, much of the garbage seen here could be reused, or recycled, to make new things. This would mean taking fewer raw materials from our environment.

4

# Do it yourself

## Do a packaging survey.

Much of the garbage we throw out comes from packaging (the materials used to wrap food and other goods we buy from stores). Next time you or a member of your family go shopping, count the number of layers of wrapping on some of the items. Packaging holds the goods together and makes them look attractive. But often you will find there are lots of unnecessary layers.

chocolate wrappers

lid

lid

tray

protective layer

paper

base

a box of chocolates may have up to six layers of packaging

cakes may have up to four layers

cellophane

cake

base

tray

box

tray

toys usually have few layers

toy

office waste

industrial waste

store waste

These are just some of the many things we think of as waste. But the real waste is throwing away so many valuable materials such as paper, glass, wood, and metals. Even kitchen waste can be reused.

today

20 years ago

## Getting Lighter

In the last 20 years, the packaging used for supermarket goods has become one-third lighter. This helps to cut down on waste and saves energy.

5

# Where Does It Go?

Each week, our garbage is put out in garbage cans to be taken away. Much of it ends up being buried in a landfill. This is a big hole in the ground, such as a disused quarry or sand pit. But burying garbage takes up a lot of space and spoils the countryside. Sometimes the garbage is taken to an incinerator where it is burned. The heat may be used to make electricity for local homes. But burning it produces harmful fumes that pollute the air.

### Energy from Waste

Burning garbage to make electricity is a useful way of getting rid of waste. One canful of garbage can generate as much electricity as a bag of coal.

Not all garbage is wasted. Rotting garbage gives off a gas called methane, which can be burned to make electricity. Kitchen and garden waste can be made into compost and sprayed on fields. And many materials can be recycled.

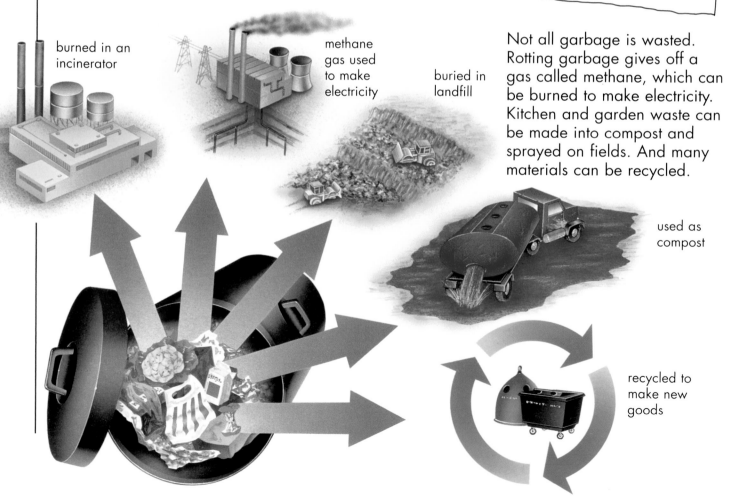

burned in an incinerator

methane gas used to make electricity

buried in landfill

used as compost

recycled to make new goods

Garbage put in a landfill is squashed down before more garbage is placed on top. Eventually, the hole is filled. Then it can be covered with soil and turned into a park or a sports field.

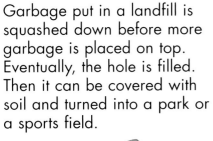

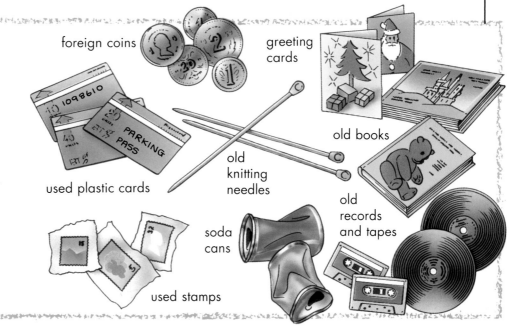

Recycling is a good way to help our planet. It saves materials, energy, and land that might otherwise be used as landfill. It also reduces pollution.

## Do it yourself

### Have a charity drive.

Charities collect a wide range of items that might otherwise get thrown away. Find out what your local charity store collects and have a charity drive at home. Instead of being burned, your waste could end up helping someone.

foreign coins

greeting cards

used plastic cards

old knitting needles

old books

used stamps

soda cans

old records and tapes

# Nature's Recycling

Have you noticed that you never see huge piles of dead trees and animals in woodlands? This is because natural materials quickly decompose (break down) and are recycled. These materials are said to be biodegradable. Nature is very good at recycling, so nothing goes to waste. Insects, earthworms, fungi, and microscopic bacteria are important because their job is to break down the wastes. They are called decomposers.

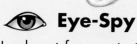 **Eye-Spy**

Look out for waste that is biodegradable. Apple cores, dead leaves, old clothes, cardboard boxes, and newspapers will all eventually rot or get eaten.

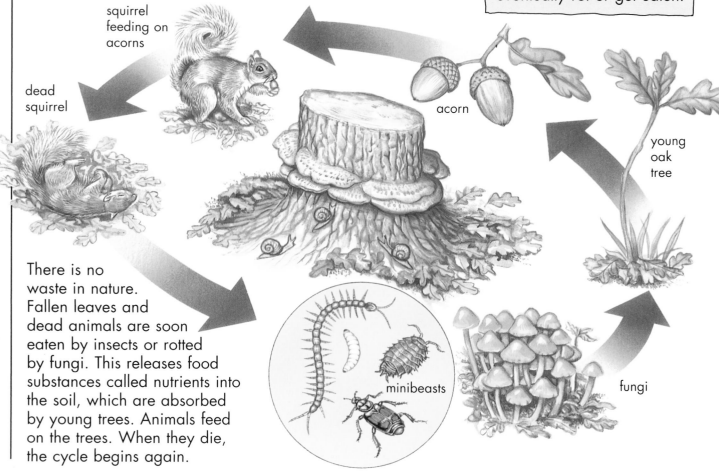

squirrel feeding on acorns

dead squirrel

acorn

young oak tree

minibeasts

fungi

There is no waste in nature. Fallen leaves and dead animals are soon eaten by insects or rotted by fungi. This releases food substances called nutrients into the soil, which are absorbed by young trees. Animals feed on the trees. When they die, the cycle begins again.

8

# Do it yourself

## Catch some insect decomposers using this simple method.

**1.** Cut a piece of thick paper about 12in. x 8in. Roll it up to make a funnel shape and tape it together. The hole at the bottom should be about $\frac{1}{2}$in. across.

folding paper into funnel

**2.** Put some damp tissue in the bottom of a glass jar and wrap the jar with a piece of black paper. Put your funnel in the jar.

**3.** Collect some leaf litter from under some trees. (Leaf litter is a damp mixture of rotten leaves and soil.)

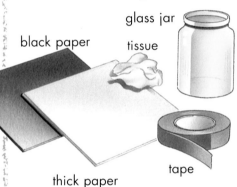

glass jar

black paper

tissue

thick paper

tape

## Worms at Work

Worms are good recyclers. They feed on dead and rotting matter, such as leaves, that they find on the ground. This helps to break the matter down so it can be reused by plants.

**4.** Fill your funnel with leaf litter and leave the jar sitting under a strong light from a table lamp for two hours. Insects prefer dark damp places, so the ones in your leaf litter will try to crawl away from the heat and light of the lamp. They will soon fall through the bottom of the funnel into the jar.

## More Things To Try

Build a home for your decomposers by turning a large jar on its side. Make breathing holes in the lid and put some soil, rotten wood, and leaf litter inside, along with your insects. Add plenty of food such as apple or potato peels and keep the soil damp. Then cover the jar with a dark cloth. Return the creatures to their natural habitat after a few days.

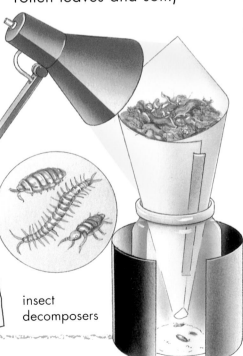

insect decomposers

decomposers' home

9

# Garbage That Won't Rot

If you left a plastic bag, a glass bottle, or an aluminum can outside, it would stay there unchanged for hundreds of years. This is because plastic, glass, and some metals are nonbiodegradable—they will never rot. Of course, it is important for some materials to be nonbiodegradable. Building materials, glass, and many plastics must stay intact to do their job properly. But when no longer needed, these materials are difficult to get rid off.

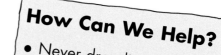

nuts          nails

Much of the garbage we throw out each week will never rot. We have to keep creating new landfill sites to take it all. One day, our planet could become one big garbage dump!

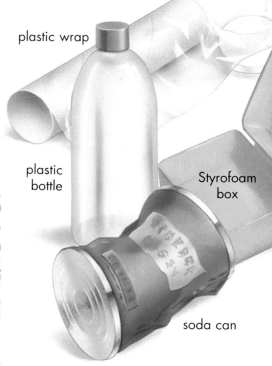

plastic wrap

plastic bottle

Styrofoam box

soda can

## Do it yourself

**Do a litter survey to find out how much litter there is in your street, around your school, and in your local park.**

Draw a chart like the one shown below. Mark on your chart how much litter you find in each place and what kind of litter it is. Clear the litter up as you go by putting it in a garbage bag. Be sure to wear gloves when you touch litter.

## How Can We Help?
- Never drop litter—garbage that is made of plastics, Styrofoam, metals, and glass will not rot away.
- Do a litter survey like the one here, and organize a "litter blitz" to clear it all up.

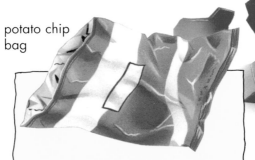
potato chip bag

glass

aluminum foil

batteries

## 👁 Eye-Spy

Because most litter does not rot, it will stay in our environment for many years unless it is cleared up. Check the dates on litter, such as potato chip bags, to see how old it is.

Litter gets everywhere, from our streets to our beaches, and it is not a pretty sight. People who drop nonbiodegradable waste outdoors are spoiling the environment for everyone else.

# Do it yourself

**Find out which garbage is biodegradable and which is not by doing this simple test.**

**1.** Collect some plastic containers and fill them with damp soil.

**2.** Find several bits of man-made garbage and several bits of natural garbage. Bury each object in a pot and identify it with a label. Leave the pots somewhere cool and damp for a couple of weeks, then dig up the objects to see if they have rotted or changed at all.

## How It Works

The natural garbage will have started to decompose or may have rotted away altogether because it is biodegradable. The man-made garbage does not decompose and will not have changed at all. Luckily, we can recycle much of our non-biodegradable garbage so that it can be used again.

plastic containers

soil

banana peel

paper

leaf

marble

nail

lid

candy wrapper

potato peel

11

# Waste Not, Want Not

It is very wasteful to throw things away if they can be reused or recycled. Raw materials have to be taken from the environment to make new things, which uses energy and causes pollution. So the more we throw away, the more the environment will be harmed. The number of materials we can recycle is increasing all the time. Once, only glass and metal were recyclable. Today, we can also recycle paper, cardboard, rags, batteries, plastics, and much more.

### 👁 Eye-Spy

Next time you empty a bottle or soda can, finish a comic book, or tear a T-shirt, think whether the leftovers can be recycled.

## Christmas Recycling

Instead of throwing out your old Christmas tree in the garbage, take it to a recycling center where you may be able to get it chipped into tiny pieces for reuse as garden compost.

**30%** wastepaper and cardboard

**30%** kitchen waste

**10%** metal

**10%** glass

**8%** plastics

**4%** old clothes

**8%** other materials, including dust

This diagram shows the different amounts of waste that get thrown out in our garbage each week. If we were more careful, we could recycle three-fourths of our household waste.

# Do it yourself

**Find out how much garbage your family produces in a week and sort it into bags ready for recycling.**

**1.** Find seven plastic bags and tape a piece of scrap paper onto each one so you can write down what it contains. You will need a bag for each of the following: metal, paper, cardboard, plastics, glass, old clothes and fabrics, and food scraps.

**2.** Sort your garbage into the different bags and see how much you collect in a week. How does your garbage compare with the amounts shown in the diagram opposite?

sorting garbage into different bags

## Nothing Wasted

The people in many poorer countries are far better at recycling than we are. They cannot afford to throw away things like plastic bags and bottles, which we take for granted. All their garbage is carefully sorted so that any useful materials can be recycled. This couple is collecting cardboard boxes for recycling in Vietnam.

## How Can We Help?

We should all try to cut down on the amount of garbage we produce. The best way to do so is to remember the three Rs— reduce, reuse, and recycle! We can reduce waste by buying less in the first place, reuse items such as plastic bags and glass jars instead of throwing them away, and recycle our garbage so that materials are not wasted.

# Gardens and Garages

A lot of recycling can be done at home. For example, biodegradable kitchen and yard waste, such as food scraps and grass cuttings, can be put on a compost heap. The waste quickly rots down to form a compost which makes a good fertilizer (food) for garden plants. Your garage may be full of old junk that usually ends up on the local garbage dump. Some of it might find a new life as a flower container or a rain barrel.

Fallen leaves can be recycled by digging them into the soil. As they rot, the leaves form a substance called humus, which makes a good plant food.

## Do it yourself

**Build a compost heap or "worm factory" for your kitchen waste so you can recycle food scraps into a rich compost that will help your plants to grow.**

**1.** Ask an adult to drill two lines of holes around the bottom of an old garbage can as shown on the opposite page. This will allow any liquid to drain out of your can.

**2.** Put a layer of gravel or rocks, about 7in. deep, in the bottom of your bin. Follow this with a layer of sand about 3in. deep. The sand and rocks will allow water to drain through your can while still keeping the contents damp.

sand

compost

earth-worms

gravel

kitchen waste

slats of wood

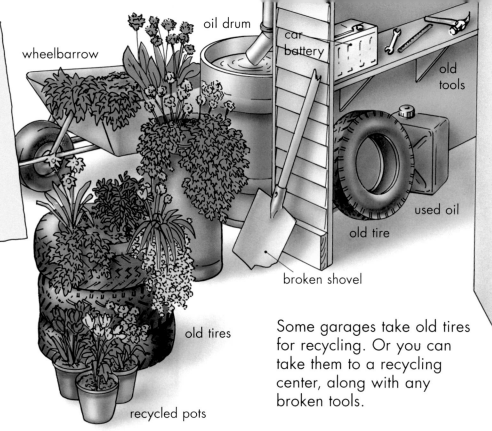

**wheelbarrow**

**oil drum**

**car battery**

**old tools**

**used oil**

**old tire**

**broken shovel**

**old tires**

**recycled pots**

Old tires and broken wheelbarrows can be recycled to make unusual flower containers. Pots are often made of recycled materials.

Some garages take old tires for recycling. Or you can take them to a recycling center, along with any broken tools.

**3.** Add a layer of wooden slats to stop the compost mixing with the sand. Put about 6in. of potting compost on top.

**4.** Buy some earthworms from a fishing shop and lay them in the compost. Feed them regularly with kitchen waste, such as fruit and vegetable peels, cabbage leaves, crushed eggshells, and cheese rinds. Do not feed them meat or fruit.

**5.** Leave the lid on your worm factory to keep it warm and damp. The compost will be ready to use on your garden after two to three months.

**6.** Pick out the worms before you put the compost on your garden. Return them to their worm factory so they can get back to work!

kitchen waste

worms in compost

wooden slats

sand

gravel

15

# Down the Drain

Every day, we each use gallons of water to clean ourselves and to flush the toilet. We also use water for cooking, and in dishwashers and washing machines, as well as for washing the car. Once we have finished with the water, it disappears down the drain. But that is not the last we see of it. It is then cleaned and recycled so we can use it again. There always seems to be plenty of fresh water. But sometimes, if there has been a drought, there is hardly enough to go around. So we must all try to reduce the amount of water we use.

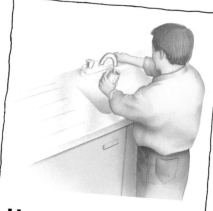

## How Many Times?

In many large cities, water from the faucet has been recycled as many as 20 times! But it is still perfectly safe to drink.

## Do it yourself

**Do a water survey to see how much water is used at home by your family in a day.**

Draw a chart like the one here, listing all the things that use up water in your home, such as flushing the toilet, or having a bath. Mark it on your chart each time someone uses water. How is water used most often? Could you think of ways to use less water?

| | How often |
|---|---|
| Water filter | ЖЖ I |
| Cooking | II |
| Washing car | I |
| Washing machine | II |
| Dishwasher | I |
| Toilet | ЖЖ |
| Bathtub | II |
| Watering plants | II |
| Sprinkler | I |

16

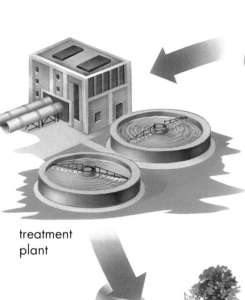

your home

treatment plant

**The Water Cycle**

reservoir supplies homes with water

rain falls

clean water pumped into river

water evaporates

Dirty water from your home goes to a treatment plant to be cleaned. Then it is poured into rivers and carried to the sea. Some water evaporates (turns into a gas) and forms clouds. When rainwater falls, it fills up the reservoirs that supply us with water.

# Do it yourself

## See how quickly water evaporates.

Measure out $\frac{1}{4}$ cup of water into each of three different containers—a saucer, a glass, and a bottle. Leave them on a sunny windowsill for a day.

From which container has most water disappeared?

## How It Works

The water evaporates fastest from the saucer because it has a large surface area open to the air. It takes longest to evaporate from the bottle because there is little surface area open to the air and only a small hole to escape through.

17

# Do it yourself

**Water is cleaned at a treatment plant by filtering it through soil, sand, and gravel to remove all the dirt. Try making your own water filter.**

**1.** Line a funnel with a coffee filter paper. Put a layer of fine sand, about $1\frac{1}{2}$ in. deep, in the bottom of the lining paper.

**2.** Mix a handful of soil with some water. Pour the dirty water into the funnel and see how well the sand filters out the soil. Does the water come out clean?

water

## How It Works

As the water trickles through the sand, pieces of dirt are trapped by the sand particles and the water is cleaned.

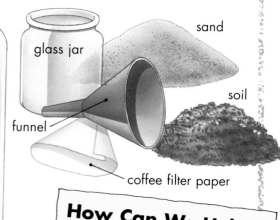

sand

glass jar

soil

funnel

coffee filter paper

## How Can We Help?

Save water—it is too precious to waste.
- Turn faucets off so they don't drip.
- Take a shower instead of a bath—you will save 7–12 gallons every time.
- Put a brick in the tank so less water is wasted when you flush the toilet.

Water containing sewage (human waste) is treated at a sewage plant (shown left). The solids are removed, then the liquid part is trickled through filter beds where bacteria break down any germs.

# Plenty of Paper

Paper is a very useful material. It is used to make books, newspapers, paper money, writing paper, magazines, and much more. Most of it is made from conifer trees. The wood is chipped into tiny pieces and mixed with water and chemicals to produce a pulp. Then it is drained, squeezed, and dried to form a huge roll of paper. Paper and cardboard are easily recycled. The old paper is chopped up and put back into the papermaking process at the pulping stage.

## Eye-Spy

A special symbol is used to show that something has been made from recycled paper. How many things can you spot in your house that have this symbol on them?

This diagram shows the different stages in making paper, from chipping, pulping, and refining to rolling and drying.

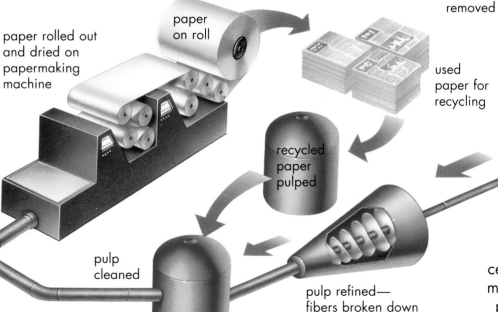

timber cut down

bark removed

wood chipped

used paper for recycling

water and chemicals added and chips pulped

paper on roll

paper rolled out and dried on papermaking machine

recycled paper pulped

pulp cleaned

pulp refined— fibers broken down

Paper taken from recycling centers is pulped and then mixed in with the ordinary pulp to make new paper.

## Why Recycle It?

Recycling paper means less garbage needs to be buried in landfills. Making new paper from old also saves on chemicals, energy, and water. But it does not really save trees because most paper is made from conifers that are grown specially for this purpose.

Paper and cardboard is tightly packed into bales, ready to be recycled. If we did not recycle our paper, we would need to cut down five million trees every day!

## How Can We Help?

- Take newspapers and cardboard to your local recycling center.
- Reuse old envelopes by putting a sticky label over the old address.
- Whenever possible, draw or write on both sides of your paper so you don't waste any.
- Collect scrap paper and staple it together to make a phone message pad.

The trees used for making paper come from conifer plantations. As trees are cut down, new trees are planted in their place, so there is a constant supply of wood. Unfortunately, the plantations replace natural habitats, such as forests, that are rich in wildlife. By recycling paper we are helping to save wildlife.

## How Much Paper?

On average, a person in the United States uses 680lbs. (310kg) of paper every year, almost twice as much as someone in England and 100 times more than in India.

U.S.A. 680lbs.
England 360lbs.
India 7lbs.

# Do it yourself

**Make some recycled paper. You will need an adult to help you.**

**1.** Tear up several newspapers into thin strips and leave them to soak in a bucket of water overnight.

**4.** Cut a piece of fine plastic mesh slightly bigger than your frame. (You can buy the mesh from a garden center. Choose a mesh with holes less than $\frac{1}{4}$ in. across.) Tack or staple the mesh onto the frame.

scooping the frame under the pulp

paper pulp

plastic bowl

saucepan

newspaper

nails

plastic mesh

hammer

tacks

wooden frame

**2.** Ask an adult to boil the mixture in an old pan for 10 minutes until the paper dissolves into a mushy stew. Leave it to cool. Then pour the mixture into a wide, flat plastic bowl.

**3.** Now ask the adult to help you make a frame that will fit into your bowl. You will need to cut four lengths of wood and nail them together at the corners.

**5.** Starting with the frame held upright, scoop it into the bucket and under the pulp that is floating on the surface of the water. Then lift the frame out flat so that there is an even layer of pulp all over it.

**6.** When the water has drained away, turn the pulp out onto a piece of felt or an old blanket. Add two more layers of pulp.

**7.** Place another piece of felt or blanket on top, then a hard board. Step on the board to squeeze out all the water, then remove the top blanket and board and leave the paper to dry.

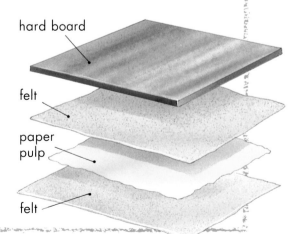

hard board

felt

paper pulp

felt

# Banks for Bottles

Glass has been used for thousands of years. It is made by heating sand, soda, and limestone together at very high temperatures so that they melt and form a liquid. As the liquid cools, it turns into glass. Glass is easy to recycle. The old glass is cleaned and broken up, then it is melted and molded into shape just like new glass. Recycling means taking fewer raw materials from the ground. It also helps to save energy.

Buying milk and orange juice in returnable glass bottles saves energy and raw materials because the bottles can be reused up to 11 times. A carton can only be used once.

crushing glass

hot glass

glass for recycling

melting glass in furnace

bottle bank

bottle mold

supermarket

filling and capping bottles

Glass from a bottle bank is cleaned and broken up into small pieces called cullet. The cullet is melted down in a furnace and the liquid glass is then poured into a mold and left to cool. The bottles are filled and capped, ready for our supermarket shelves.

A mountain of glass lies waiting to be recycled. Glass is sorted into different colors before it is processed. Clear glass is the most useful because it can be made into all kinds of bottles and jars, but green glass has fewer uses—it is mostly made into wine bottles.

# Do it yourself

**Instead of recycling it, reuse a glass bottle to make this pretty table decoration.**

**1.** Buy a block of florists' foam from a flower shop and cut off a small piece about 3in. square and 1½in. deep.

**2.** Cut a hole in the middle big enough to fit over the neck of the bottle. Soak the foam in water, then put it over the neck. Now place a candle in the bottle and fill the foam with pretty flowers and ivy. (Do not light the candle without an adult present.)

glass bottle

florist's foam

flowers

candle

## How Can We Help?

- Take unwanted glass to a bottle bank to be recycled.
- Buy milk, orange juice, and soda pop in reusable glass bottles rather than cartons and plastic bottles whenever possible.
- Reuse bottles and jars as containers or vases (see below for ideas).

bathroom tiles

reflective street signs

fiberglass kayak

bricks

Not all recycled glass is used to make new bottles and jars. Some is used to make bathroom tiles, bricks, reflective road signs, and fiberglass boats and kayaks.

# Do it yourself

### Make a bottle orchestra.

Collect some empty bottles and jars of all shapes and sizes and wash them out. Fill them with different amounts of water to give a range of notes, then "play" them by tapping them with a metal spoon. See if you can play any tunes you know.

playing bottle with metal spoon

## More Things To Try

Reuse glass bottles and jars by turning them into containers for pens and pencils, flowers, marbles, and much more. Paint them with crazy designs or glue paper scraps or stamps all over them.

# Cans Count

Metal food cans have been used for about 200 years. Cans are ideal for storing food and drink for long periods. We use millions of them every day. The metal used in cans is valuable, so recycling is very important. There is no limit to the number of times the metal can be recycled. Steel made from old cans uses just one-fourth of the energy that would be needed to make steel from raw materials. Recycling also means digging up fewer raw materials, creating less garbage, and filling up fewer landfills.

## What to Recycle?

All sorts of metal items can be recycled, including steel and aluminum food and soda cans, bottle tops, and aluminum foil and frozen food trays.

## Cans in Space

Every year, billions of cans are used in the United States alone. If they were lined up end to end, they would stretch to the Moon and back many times!

Everything made of steel contains some steel that has been recycled. The steel in a can of beans could end up in a bridge, a car, a knife, or just a simple paper clip.

cutlery

scissors

refrigerators

kitchen knives

bridges

paper clips

cars

## Aluminum and Steel Cans

The first cans were made from iron coated with a thin layer of tin, which is why we still call them tin cans. Nowadays, cans are made from steel or aluminum. Soda cans have to be light, so they are made from a very thin sheet of metal. Food cans have to be thicker and stronger so they can protect their contents.

### 👁 Eye-Spy

Most soda cans now have a symbol, or logo, on their side, reminding you to recycle them. Here are some of the logos to look out for.

Inside a recycling plant special machines are used to squash aluminum cans into bales. The cans are then melted down and rolled out to form sheet aluminum, ready to be used again.

## Do it yourself

**Do this simple test to see if a can is made of steel or aluminum.**

Steel is magnetic—that is, it is attracted to magnets—and aluminum is not. So hold the can up to a magnet and see if it sticks. If it does, it is made of steel. If it does not, it is made of aluminum.

Check other metal objects to see if they are magnetic, such as needles, keys, pencil sharpeners, knives, foil, and bottle tops. If they are, they are made of steel or iron.

magnet

can

## Saving Energy

The amount of energy needed to make one aluminum can from raw materials is the same as that required to make 20 cans from recycled aluminum.

## How Can We Help?

- Take empty food and soda cans to your local recycling center.
- Encourage your school to get a can bank so you can all collect cans for recycling.
- Don't forget that foil, bottle tops, and frozen food trays can be recycled too!

## Do it yourself

**Use a couple of empty food cans and a length of string to make your own "mobile phone."**

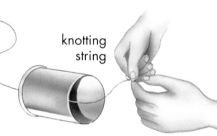

food cans

nail

hammer

knotting string

string

**1.** Ask an adult to file down any sharp edges on the cans. Then wash them out.

**2.** With an adult's help, make a hole in each can, in the center of the base, using a hammer and nail.

**3.** Cut a piece of string 65 feet long. Feed each end through a hole in the base of the cans. Tie the ends off with a knot on the inside.

**4.** Ask a friend to hold a can up to his or her ear and stand as far away from you as possible. Keeping the string pulled tight, speak into your can and see if your friend can hear you.

## How It Works

Your voice makes the can vibrate as you speak into it. The vibrations are carried along the string to the other can which also vibrates, reproducing the sound of your voice so your friend can hear you speaking.

27

# Recycling Plastics

Plastic is a very useful material that is cheap and easy to make. This is why we use so much of it. In the United States, two and a half million plastic bottles are used every hour! Most plastic is non-biodegradable, which makes it difficult to get rid of. The best way is to recycle it and make something new with it. Oil is used to make many plastics, so recycling also saves oil.

Record discs are made from plastic. There are millions of unwanted records in the world now being collected and made into credit cards!

stuffing for furnishings

garbage bags

pipe

pots

fencing

boots

bottles

shopping bags

## Eye-Spy

These logos are used on plastic packaging to show that it can be recycled. A different number is used for each type of plastic. Can you find these logos on containers in your home?

A surprising range of objects can be made using recycled plastic, from bags and bottles to boots, pots, and pipes.

# Do it yourself

**Reuse a plastic bottle to make an unusual plant holder. You may need to ask an adult to help you with the cutting.**

**1.** Find an empty 64oz. plastic soda bottle and peel off the label. Using a felt-tip pen, draw two rings around the bottle, one 3in. from the bottom, the other 5in. from the top as shown on the page opposite.

plastic soda bottle

scissors

small plant

## Fast Food

Styrofoam fast-food containers trap the heat so that the food does not get cold. They once had to be thrown away, but now they can be recycled.

Plastics for recycling are first sorted into the different types. Then they are washed and shredded into tiny pieces, or chips, before being melted down and turned into something new.

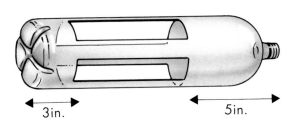

3in.          5in.

**2.** Draw two lines, $\frac{3}{4}$ in. apart, down the length of the bottle between the two rings. Draw three more sets of lines, evenly spacing them around the bottle. Cut out the large rectangles between your lines.

**3.** Make two holes in the top of the bottle and thread string through to hang up your container. Finally, put a small plant inside.

## How Can We Help?

- Take plastic bottles and other packaging to your local recycling center.
- Take an old plastic bag with you when you go shopping so you don't need to be given a new one.
- Reuse plastic ice cream tubs as sandwich or freezer boxes.
- Use yogurt containers to mix paint or glue in.

29

# Recycle Your Rags

Old clothes and rags should never be thrown away. Just like glass and paper, rags can be recycled. Some fabrics are ripped up to make a substance called "shoddy." This is used to make furniture fabrics, blankets, carpets, and even new clothes. Other fabrics are turned into stuffing for mattresses, and some are used as wiping cloths for machinery.

### New from Old

This girl is wearing an outfit knitted entirely out of recycled wool.

Some old clothes are collected by charities and are resold or sent to poorer countries. A few clothes are burned as garbage. But the rest can be recycled.

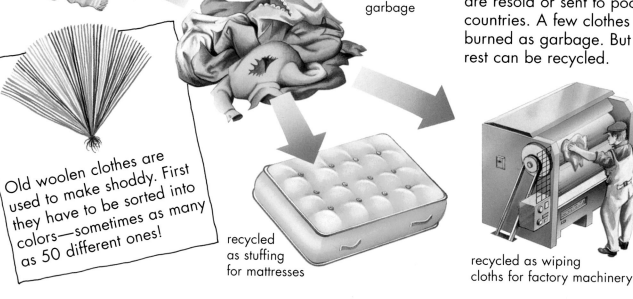

recycled as blankets, furnishing fabrics, carpets, and clothes

sent to people in poor countries

burned as garbage

Old woolen clothes are used to make shoddy. First they have to be sorted into colors—sometimes as many as 50 different ones!

recycled as stuffing for mattresses

recycled as wiping cloths for factory machinery

# Do it yourself

**Turn an old sock into a fun puppy puppet. You could even make lots of different animals and put on your own puppet show.**

**1.** Find an old sock and sew up any holes.

**2.** Using a felt-tip pen, draw two ears, two eyes, a nose, and a tongue onto brightly colored felt or cotton fabric. Copy the shapes given here, making them as big as you like. Or draw different shapes and make a mouse, a cat, or some other animal.

**3.** Now glue or sew all the different shapes onto your sock.

**4.** To use your puppet, put your hand inside the sock so that the heel sits over your knuckles. Push the toe in on itself to form the mouth. Then tap your fingers and thumb together to make your puppet "talk."

tongue

pointed ear

eye

nose

floppy ear

31

# Index